WALKING THE LOG

MEMORIES OF A
SOUTHERN CHILDHOOD

Paintings and stories by

Bessie Nickens

RIZZOLI
NEW YORK

I was born in Sligo, Louisiana, in 1906. I first started school when I was seven years old, because in Vivian, Louisiana, where I first lived, there were no schools for blacks. When we went to Fullerton, Louisiana, my sister and I started school. My whole family always moved around. For a time we stayed with my grandmother while my mother and father worked in the oil fields.

Then we went to Conroe, Texas—I hated it when my mother moved from there because they had a college, and I wanted to go to college. But we had nothing then, we lived in a little old shack, and I think I had two dresses, one on the line and one on my back. We didn't have a dresser, we just had a mirror and box, a stove, no rugs on the floor. But we had plenty to eat, and plenty of milk to drink.

When I was young, I liked to be by myself. That's when I started tracing in an old Sears, Roebuck catalog. I was about seven. I traced for a long time before I started drawing freehand, and then I didn't have to trace anymore. Then I got Crayolas, and I would use the Crayolas to make pictures. If you rub your hand over Crayolas long enough they'll shine just like oil. And then I heard some-body say something about oil, so I got some oil paint and I taught myself to use it. You have to mix it with turpentine. That turpentine was strong! It wasn't odorless like it is now. And then I heard about pastels, and I started doing pastels.

When we moved to Dallas, Texas, I was good at drawing by then. I won a prize for drawing a boy on crutches. And then I sold a painting—I painted some red roses on some satin. I remember I sold it for a dollar. It was a beautiful thing, but I didn't have any money so I sold it.

I just started really painting since I retired. I am now eighty-eight years old. I've been painting for the last three years. I paint regularly, every day, day and night. More than ever. When I get through with one painting, I just think of my childhood and then I paint some more.

Each picture I paint has its own story, and they're all different. Some of the pictures tell about the times we all picked cotton. Other paintings show how we lived when my father worked in the lumber mills. The pictures and stories in this book move around just as much as I did when I was growing up. It's what I remember. Each picture has its own story.

Bessie Nickens

We went to church every Sunday morning. My grandfather was
the Deacon and he opened up the service every Sunday with
prayer and singing.

In those days, there were no cars or anything like that. People
came to church on horseback, in buggies, wagons, and, of
course, those that were near the church walked. We walked.
You see, all the black people, more or less, the majority of
them were sharecroppers. They wouldn't own the buggies,
but their landlord would let them use them.

Now, we children didn't play when we went to church. We sat
there with the other people. You knew not to talk, because
if you started talking or doing something that you were not
supposed to do, all the old people just looked at you and when
you got that look you knew to sit down and be quiet. I never
had my grandfather look at me like that because I always loved
him, so I knew what to do and what not to do. My grandfather
was an angel. If anybody went to heaven, he did. He was a
beautiful, clean man, and I loved him.

When we went to church, we had on our Sunday clothes. Oh yes,
we had our little calico dresses on. The men were in suits, just
like in the painting. They may not have had but one suit, but
they had that. All men wore hats, they didn't go bareheaded
then. And women wore hats to church. Everybody wore hats.

My mother loved flowers, and I did, too. We had flowers, many flowers around the house. Mama would put them into jars. I always liked flowers in my room.

We picked wildflowers everywhere—there were always wildflowers out in the country. There were daisies and sunflowers and lots and lots of morning glories. Everywhere we went we'd go picking wildflowers. We'd pick them to have something to do I guess.

Butterflies—I intended to put a butterfly in the painting, but I didn't. We'd catch butterflies and we used to catch a lot of grasshoppers, too. Get up on them and catch them right quick. You have to be real quick because they'll get away from you. We just caught them for fun. Sometimes you'd catch a whole bunch of butterflies. We'd catch them with our hands. You can catch them if there's a lot of them because sometimes butterflies go together almost like geese. They bunch up and fly together. Some of them would be really big. I'm going to paint that one day.

Rabbits were all around everywhere. Rabbits and squirrels. We'd see them, but we didn't kill them. Every now and then there was a snake. There were a lot of green grass snakes, but they would always run from us. I remember one time I stepped across a snake before I ever saw him. And— oooh!—I was scared! It was in the spring and it was cool and he had just come out of hibernation. When they first come out they're almost immobile. That's the only reason I think I didn't get bitten. I stepped across that snake and I was barefoot! Oooh, I was scared! I'm going to paint that one of these days—I'm going to have my head *that* big and my eyes *that* big. It happened when I was about seven, but it seems like it was yesterday.

This area was nothing but trees, just hundreds and hundreds of
dogwood trees with those beautiful white blossoms. All kinds
of pretty flowers would grow out where this creek was. I think
it must have been a swamp, because calla lilies would grow
there, and blackberries and muscadine. We would walk
through these woods, this thick, wooded area, we'd walk
through there barefooted. I wouldn't do that now for nothing!
And this log had fallen across this creek, and we walked that
log. This was fun to us. And of course our little dog Polo would
walk the log with us.

We'd roam within a mile or so of our house, just walking in the
woods, having fun, catching grasshoppers and butterflies.
We just walked all around, climbed trees, picked flowers and
fruits. There was muscadine, it looks like a grapevine running
up a tree, we'd pick those grapes and eat them. There were
also mahoe trees—they had little bitty things that looked like
an apple. We'd eat them right off the tree. That water in the
creek was clear and beautiful, it wasn't polluted like it is today.
You could get down there and drink right out of that creek.

Birds were out there, and squirrels and rabbits. Lots of birds. See
the one over there, on the tree? That's a woodpecker. Have you
ever seen a woodpecker? Isn't it funny how he can cut that
wood with his beak?

I used to sit down in the woods sometimes by myself and just listen
to the birds sing and the sounds of the creek. I loved to sit by a
creek and just meditate by myself. Have you ever done that?
I've done it all my life.

We lived in that old house near the creek. Mama would get the clothes and the tubs and the kids would take it all down near the creek and carry the water from the creek to that iron tub there. You put a fire under it and boiled your white clothes. And then when you got all your things clean you would hang them on the line with clothespins. If we didn't have enough line we'd hang clothes on the bushes to dry.

That was an old shack, it had about three rooms. We didn't have a living room, nothing like that. It had a kitchen and two bedrooms and a stove and we stayed in the kitchen for heat. No fireplace.

We didn't have all those beautiful flowers and things in this area. No dogwood trees or nothing like that, just plain old trees. I just remember that washing scene. And that house, I remember that was an old unpainted shack, as usual.

I remember being lonely around here. There were no kids in this area that I recall. That was right out in the woods. Just miles and miles of this timber. I don't remember anybody else around there. So it was a little bit lonely because I only had my brother and sister to play with.

When we played hide and go seek, it was three of us—my brother, my sister, and me—and then some neighborhood children.

If you were it, you waited until you thought everybody was hid and then you called out, "All hid." See, in the painting she's hollering, "All hid." If nobody says nothing, she calls out, "All ain't hid holler big fat hen!" And if you weren't hid yet you called out, "Big Fat Hen!"

I'd hide anywhere I could find to hide if somebody else wasn't there. You see where the kids are hidden? See, there's one in the barn. There's one down behind the bushes, there's one up behind the hog pen, and there's one behind the outhouse. And there's another one behind the white house, and then there's one behind the cow, and there's another one by the tree. Oh, here's another one behind the horse.

The owner of the house was named Mr. Newby, and this is where he lived. We lived in a house in back of his; he was the land-owner. He was really a good man; he let us play all around his house. Now he had pigs and cows and chickens and hogs and all that sort of thing. My grandfather took care of all of that, did all the work. Sharecropping. I love my grandfather to this day. He was a wonderful, beautiful man. I never saw him show anger, no matter what.

Mrs. Newby was a doll of a woman. She was so good to us, she used to let my sister and me come up to the house, and she taught me how to crochet, taught me how to knit, and taught me how to tat. I had real long hair and she used to buy me beautiful ribbons.

D O U B L E   D U T C H

I remember jumping rope in Conroe, Texas. That girl jumping was our neighbor there. I remember her, her name was Exie. She was tough, like a tomboy. I guess she must have been about thirteen or fourteen years old, but she looked older. She was tall. And she was tough.

Double rope, I called it. Some people called it double dutch. I never got in there. See, that's fast. My sister used to throw the rope. I never could even do that. They're throwing that rope *fast*. And you had to jump both of them. But old Exie used to do it. We used to just play it with girls. I never did see the boys jump.

We played jacks, ring around the rosy, the whip, hopscotch. I was good at jacks, and I liked to play ring around the rosy. I didn't like those tough games, like jumping rope and snap the whip. I liked hide and go seek. I loved that. And hopscotch, I liked that, too.

And we always played baseball. Girls and boys played together. Yes, that's one thing we used to play all the time, you know, sandlot baseball. We all played the same thing, boys and girls mixed in.

GIRL ON THE ROPE SWING

That's the way I swung all the time. I loved to swing. Wherever we went, we'd always find a tree that we'd put a rope on. Just tie it on there. Someone, Mama or somebody, would push to get you started. That's my Mama there. She'd watch me swing. I think I liked to swing better than my brother and sister did, because I was always on it. I'd go as high as I could! You know, once you get started, you push yourself. You'd go *wayyy* up and come back *wayyy* up.

You know when you're swinging high like that, with a good fresh breeze, you really enjoy that. I loved it. When I was doing that swinging, I was happy.

There's my little doggy, Polo. And that's my cat, Bessiecat. Only cat I ever had.

In those days they had what you call a quilting bee. Ladies didn't have to go out to work like they do now, and they would all get together and put a quilt on a rack and they would all get around it and quilt, helping each other, you know, helping some neighbor finish her quilt. And then they would serve tea, coffee, and tea cakes. It was more or less a social thing.

I never quilted, and I never did get to learn. I didn't even learn how to sew until I was grown. My mother was an excellent seamstress and my sister was an excellent seamstress. They never let me do anything like that. Whenever I'd get up to do something, like sew or do my math, my sister always said, "I'll do it!" That's why I never learned math. She was good in math. But when I needed to do my problems she'd call out, "I'll do it!" She worked all the problems. Did all the sewing.

Mama had a lot of beautiful quilts. Yes, she had a red, white, and blue one like the one in the picture. Nearly all women wore dustcaps back then. Mama wore hers every day. I was reading that a lot of women in England have those dustcaps. Most of the women I saw back then wore either a dustcap or a bonnet. I think they got that from the English ladies. Mama never wore bonnets very much, but I remember her wearing that cap. She made it herself.

SNAP THE WHIP

This was in Conroe, Texas. The kids would line up and pick a leader and he'd pull the line up and down, up and down and back and forth, and you had to hang on. The neighborhood boys and girls played together, all mixed up. I put myself in the picture, but I'm telling you, it was tough, holding on. If you let go, you were out of the game. I got in that whip once, and I didn't get in there again.

The reason I remember Conroe so well is that all the houses were painted white—all of them. Some of the people owned their houses. Some of those people were doing real good. I went to one of those houses one time and back then if you had a sewing machine, a dresser, and a piano you were considered rich. And I went to somebody's house and they had all of that, but we didn't have it.

That's my dog Polo. I still love him. Oh, Polo went everywhere we went. Old Polo was a mean dog and he would tackle any dog. He did not like other dogs. We used to say we never have seen a dog that crazy. He'd tackle a big dog! And he was a small dog! He'd run up to a big dog and tackle him and sometimes he'd get beaten all up, and we'd have to nurse him back to health. But he went everywhere we went. He loved us. Yes, Ol' Polo loved us. Ol' Polo was tough.

DOODLEBUG

A doodlebug is just a little bug. In sandy areas, you put your head close to the sand and you said,
"Doodlebug, doodlebug, yer house on fire!" And a little bug appeared, a doodlebug. We kids, my
brothers and sisters and neighbors, a bunch of us would get together and go out and just call them
up. We never did touch them.

You'd get close, see like the little boy is? You'd get close down there and you'd say, "Dooooodlebug,
doodlebug, doodlebug, yer house on fire!" And first you'd see the sand shake, and then in a few
minutes he would appear, just a little tiny bug. I never have called in the sand where one didn't
come up. It has to be sandy, though, and it has to be dry, and a bright, sunny day. I used to wonder
what made them do that. I knew he didn't understand English, so how did he know to come up?
But afterwards, I thought the vibrations from my voice must have made him come up.

And of course we all used to fly kites. My brother made kites—that's him there flying one. All the
neighborhood kids made kites. They were made out of newspaper. You'd get some sticks and cross
them up, and stick the paper on there. Sometimes my brother and I would fly a kite together.

19

COMPANY HOUSES

Now, these houses were right out in the woods. There were no towns nearby. The company had to put
up houses for their employees, because there was nothing out there. All the houses were painted the
same colors—white and red. Where we lived in this little area, there were a lot of goats. When you
hung your clothes on the line, you'd have to watch them because the goats would eat them. They
weren't wild—they just roamed the neighborhood. They weren't vicious, but they'd eat your clothes
off the line and they'd come in the house if you left your door open.

When we went to school, we walked straight down the railroad track, about a couple of miles, to a one-
room schoolhouse. We'd walk every day and come back every evening. One teacher taught up to
the sixth grade. Just one teacher. One bunch of kids would be sitting in this area in this grade, and
another bunch in another area in that grade. When she was teaching you, the other kids were studying.
They'd be quiet, she had everything under control. I liked school. I always wanted to learn. When
I was a child, I wanted to be a professional. I wanted to be a schoolteacher, that's the only thing I
knew I wanted to be. That was about the only professional job that black people did at the time,
teaching school.

S A T U R D A Y   N I G H T   B A T H

The Saturday night bath was universal. Everywhere we went we didn't have running water, so in the morning when you got up you washed your face, brushed your teeth, combed your hair. Of course in the summertime, when we went barefoot, everybody had to wash their feet at night. On the weekends, everybody would bathe. We had a big pan, see there in the picture? Everybody had a big pan back in those days. You put the big pan of water on top of the stove because the tea kettle wasn't big enough. I painted more water in that tub than they usually had.

Mama had to teach us all how to bathe, wash our necks and our ears. She saw to it that you got those feet washed, because she always said, "You don't have anything but you're goin' to sleep clean." My mother was immaculate—she was a clean woman.

Now, that soap, that was homemade soap. They made it from grease and lye. It cleaned you, too. You saved the grease left over from frying bacon and then—I don't know exactly how they did it, but they made soap with lye and grease mixed together. And then it set and they'd cut it in squares. And when you took a bath with it, you couldn't tell it was made with bacon grease and lye.

21

Nearly everywhere you went in the South they had these markets. They didn't have stores and things like they do now. There were markets everywhere. We used to get chickens there. You'd go and pick out the chicken that you wanted. I think they had somebody to pluck it for you, but you'd have to cut it up yourself. Sometimes people just took the chicken as it was, then they went home and did it up themselves. You know how to pluck a chicken? Put it in boiling water and then you pick the feathers off of it. We'd go to the market about once a week. You'd buy eggs, chickens; the little baby chickens, they're called "bitties." You could buy those if you wanted to start raising chickens. Mama used to buy a lot of little bitties and raise them up. I thought they were so cute. I did.

Mama would take her basket to the market. You didn't have any sacks. Everybody had a basket in those days. All women had baskets to go to the market or the grocery store or wherever they went.

I went to the market only once. Mama didn't take us often. I never saw any children there. Only the grownups went. I never did see people, older people, take children shopping back then. When Mama would go get our shoes, she wouldn't take us with her. She just got a string and measured our feet and brought the shoes back. Whether you liked them or not you wore them.

FLAT IRON

My mother always washed on Tuesday and ironed on Wednesday. She'd put the iron on top of this
furnace. Then she'd take the iron and wipe it off on the bag there and then she'd iron. This was the
kitchen. Mama would always put up fruit, sometimes beans and potatoes and stuff like that. We
didn't have an icebox, so when you cooked, you just cooked enough for two days.

There was no ready-made bread—you had to make your own every morning. For meals, Mama would
boil greens, collard greens, mustard greens, cabbage, beans; sometimes we'd have black-eyed peas
one day, navy beans the next day, lima beans the next day. You couldn't buy any cookies anywhere,
so in those days they made tea cakes. Every time I'd tell her to make some tea cakes, she'd make
them. I'd say, "Bessie wants tea cakes," and she'd make me some.

Back then you had dinner about twelve or one o'clock, so you ate your big meal early in the day—your
cabbage and your corn bread, and we always had dessert. Mama would make peach cobbler, apple
cobbler, or sweet potato cobbler. If she didn't have that, we'd have bread pudding. My mother could
make some of the best bread pudding. I don't know how she made it, but I thought it was delicious.

H O T   C O M B

Here my mother is doing my sister's hair. They'd get all those curls out with that hot comb. Back then
there were no beauty shops that we knew about. Madam Walker came out with the hot comb.
The comb was made out of metal and it had a little piece that went across the top of the lamp to
hold the comb—the comb would get hot, and then you'd put oil on your hair—see that jar of Poro
oil on the table? And then you'd run that hot comb through your hair to straighten it. This invention
came from Madam Walker, the first black millionaire.

We always had some books around the house, a Bible and Poor Richard's Almanack and a doctor's book,
and we had a lot of Edgar Rice Burroughs books. I used to love his Tarzan books. Mama knew I liked
them and she'd get me one every now and then. I liked the way Tarzan would swing from tree to tree
and how he could handle those animals and they could understand him and he said "wooooooooo-
oooooo," that yell. I used to imagine I could hear him yelling, his voice going through the forest.

My mother taught me how to read when I was seven. I'm still a reader. That's where I learned to paint,
by reading. I have a lot of art books, because that's the way I learned to really get into painting.

I started picking cotton when I was around ten or eleven years old. I found no joy in picking cotton—that hot sun coming down on your back all day long. Picking cotton breaks your back. And the cotton has stickers on it, burrs on it, and it just pricks your fingers. You had to be out there all day long from sunup to sundown and the only time you got any rest was at twelve o'clock, when you'd eat dinner.

When you got your sack full, you'd go and weigh it. See that scale there? And then you dumped it on the wagon. They paid thirty-five cents for every hundred pounds. My mother could pick three hundred. She could pick more than Dad.

Now, you picked cotton from early fall until the middle of November. I always missed a grade because when we got back to school it was too late for us to pass. We got way behind going on those cotton picks. My mother didn't realize the value of an education at that time. That's why I went to school so long— I was twenty-one years old before I got out of high school, but I was determined to get a high school education. The school thought I was eighteen.

And you'd live in just an old shack house, you know. The last time we were on a cotton pick, you could look up and see the sky through the roof. When it would rain, everybody would have to get over in the corner. It had a roof, but the shingles were off where it leaked. On one cotton pick there were four families in one room. Every family had a corner to sleep in. We'd take quilts and things to sleep on.

This was our last cotton pick. I was a happy soul when I was
   going home! Oh yes, I was very happy when I was going home,
   because I wanted to get back to school, I wanted to finish
   school. I *liked* school. I always wanted to go to college. As
   soon as we got back to the city, I'd get ready to go to school.
   Mama would make us some new clothes.

I didn't know it was our last cotton pick, but the next year,
   my sister told my mother she wasn't going back. So Mama
   didn't go. And I was glad of it, I'm telling you. I hated that
   cotton patch.

My sister just never could pick cotton. I could pick, I'd do pretty
   good. Some people can pick cotton, some people can't. You
   see, I would work hard because Mama wanted us to pick all
   we could, and I wanted to try to please her. But my sister didn't
   care if she was pleased or not. She always did exactly like she
   wanted to do. One day Mama told her to make some biscuits.
   My sister made the biscuits but she didn't put any baking
   powder in them and they came out just as hard as a rock.
   And she whispered to me, "I bet she won't ask me to make
   them any more." And Mama didn't. But I had to make biscuits
   every morning. She put the job off on me.

Here I am in my studio, studying about what I'm going to paint, thinking about what colors I would like to have. Sometimes when I sit down to paint I don't know exactly what's coming out. Like in *Hide And Go Seek,* I said to myself, "I'm going to paint a picture of hide and go seek," but I didn't know what I was going to put on there at the beginning. When I started painting I said, "Well, I want to make a country scene," so I said, "Well, a country scene, people have horses, they have pigs, they have chickens." So then I put the horse there and the pigs there and the chickens. But I didn't know how it was going to look. And then I said, "Well, a farm always has a barn," so then I stuck the barn over there. So you see, that's the way I do it. I just sit and think it up.

I love painting. Painting is really fascinating when you can create something yourself, something that you like. I paint what I like. Like the sunflower on page 2. When I went over and bought this sunflower, they had them on sale for a dollar. It was so pretty. They usually cost more than a dollar, but they were beginning to get old, and the man was getting rid of them for a dollar apiece at the market. I thought the leaves were so pretty, I got one. I thought it was so beautiful. And I came back home and painted it. The other sunflower in the picture, the one at the bottom, it's the same sunflower. I just turned it a little in a different direction, and painted it again. I'm going to make a picture with three sunflowers. This summer when they come out again I'm going to buy some and make a picture of three of them together.

For my grandfather, Jeff Jackson

GLOSSARY

crochet, a kind of needlework made of looped stitches
formed with a single thread and a hooked needle.

Deacon, an officer in a church, often a layperson elected
by the church to conduct services or other church
duties.

doodlebug, the larva of the ant lion, an insect that digs
a small pit in sandy soil, and waits to prey on other
insects, like ants.

icebox, an old style of refrigerator; a cabinet with a com-
partment for a large block of ice to keep food cool.

immaculate, spotlessly clean.

immobile, not able to move.

lye, a strong alkaline liquid made from wood ashes
and used in making soap and washing.

mahoe, a tropical tree with a small fruit.

muscadine, a kind of grape found in the southern
United States.

sharecropping, working as a farmer, often living on a
landowner's farm; the sharecropper gets a set amount
of money in exchange for work when the harvest
comes in.

tat, a kind of needlework used to make delicate lace,
made by looping and knotting a single cotton thread.

tea cake, a light, flat cake, like a cookie.

turpentine, an oil derived from trees that is used as a
thinner for oil paints.

First published in the United States of America in 1994 by
Rizzoli International Publications, Inc.
300 Park Avenue South
New York, New York 10010

Library of Congress Cataloging-in-Publication Data
Nickens, Bessie, 1906–
Walking the log: memories of a Southern childhood/paintings and
stories by Bessie Nickens.
p. cm.
ISBN 0-8478-1794-6
1. Nickens, Bessie, 1906– —Childhood and youth—Juvenile
literature. 2. Afro-Americans—Biography—Juvenile literature.
3. Artists—United States—Biography—Juvenile literature.
4. Afro-American artists—Biography—Juvenile literature.
5. Afro-Americans—Southern States—Social life and customs—
1865– —Juvenile literature. [1. Nickens, Bessie, 1906–
—Childhood and youth. 2. Artists. 3. Afro-Americans—Biography.
4. Southern States—Social life and customs.]
I. Title.
E185.97.N53A3 1994
973'.0496'0092—dc20
[B]
94-10803
CIP
AC

Edited by Manuela Soares and David Eli Brown

Designed by Lisa Mangano

Printed in Singapore